changing of the tides
& OTHER POEMS

changing of the Tides

& OTHER POEMS

EMMA CONLON

Written in the United States of America

ISBN 9781073100774

http://byemmaconlon.wordpress.com

instagram: @byemmaconlon
facebook: @byemmaconlon
tumblr: @emmaconlon

for all those battling the tides—
may they turn in your favor.

preface

In 2018, I was riding on a bus across my college campus when inspiration struck. I hastily pulled out a notebook and began to write with an intensity unlike anything I had ever felt before—cliché, I know. The words spilled out of me faster than I could write. In that 15 minute bus ride, I wrote a poem I impulsively titled "changing of the tides". I expected that I would change the title later; I was (and still am) prone to giving poems working titles before I finished them—only once they felt complete would I bestow them with a final, more polished title.

I did not expect this little poem to fundamentally alter the course of my life.

Reader, let me come clean: I did not think this collection of poems would ever be published. I wrote the bulk of these poems between the fall of 2018 and spring of 2020, though some exist in earlier forms stretching back to hastily scribbled lines in the margins of my high school notebooks and long abandoned blogs. As I wrote the first version of "changing of the tides" on that mundane bus ride, the pieces started to fall into place. I had a story, and I knew exactly how I wanted to tell it. This poem was the first lone drop that would soon become the ocean that is this poetry collection. With this newborn poem, I embarked on a journey to tell the stories that have lived in my notebooks and scattered dreams.

I continued working on this collection all through 2019 in my junior and senior year of college. By December, I knew I would soon be ready to publish. I set my goal publication date for right after my college graduation in May, and I waited.

When the world fell apart in 2020, my plans for this collection fell apart too. I decided to put off publishing until later that year, hoping things would get better quickly. I selected a few poems from the collection and released them in a chapbook in August as a sort of compromise. I promised myself I would get around to publication sometime that year. Then, as it is known to do, life got in the way. The months slipped away. 2020 drifted into 2021; the collection remained unpublished.

In all that time, I have let this finished collection of poetry occupy a small corner in the back of my mind as the world pressed on. I graduated, started my first job post-college, and left after a year to pursue my graduate degree so I could finally realize my dream of teaching English. Occasionally, the guilt would gnaw on the edges of my consciousness as I moved through the motions of my life. I continued to write new poems, but I decided against publishing. I felt this collection reflected a past version of myself, a skin I have since shed as I have continued to grow into adulthood. However, I now know I was wrong. These poems may not reflect the person I am currently, but they certainly represent multitudes of my past selves. I believe I owe it to the version of me who wrote these poems to finally tell the stories she could only dream of telling.

So, I present to you this little book. In honor of the poem that first inspired me to begin sharing my writing, I have titled this collection *Changing of the Tides & Other Poems*. No matter how many titles I have considered in the years since I began writing this collection, only this one felt right. I brainstormed and made endless lists of potential titles to no avail. I have relented, if only to remain true to my original intention, the scrap of an idea that whispered its way into being as I steadied my hand against the jostling of a campus bus. When I accidentally stumbled into writing this collection on that afternoon in 2018, it felt right to title the forthcoming collection after the poem that started it all. Even as I have changed over the years, the title still feels like a perfect fit.

Thank you for taking a chance on this book as it finally sees the light of day. Thank you for holding this piece of my heart in your hands. Thank you for reading.

With love and overwhelming gratitude,

Emma

contents

content warning: the *low tide* section of this book contains references to anxiety and depression.

skip it if you need to. please take care of yourself.

changing of the tides

you buried me
at the bottom of the sea,
settled the sand and smoothed the sea floor
as if to erase me. as if to silence me.
you set me adrift
in the turbulence of stormy seas
and now I float aimlessly in the aftermath,
lungs swollen with saltwater tears,
bruised and battered by the wake.
but I can see the sunlight
dabbling through the waves.

through high tides, low tides,
neaps & springs, I know. *I know.*

the tides will turn again for me.
and so they will for you.
and so they will for us.

emma conlon

high tide

emma conlon

coronation

at daybreak,
I watch the light
slink over the horizon,
dribbling watercolor streams

onto the sky's
waiting canvas, glittering
in the rolling emerald sea.
the balmy oranges and pinks

bleed around
the sun's golden halo,
like the ink that runs
from a letter read in the rain.

I am alone—
or perhaps not—
the scuttling of sand crabs
serves to remind me I am not

the only one to bear witness
to this coronation of a new day.
the sun yawns, her outstretched rays
lapping at the shimmering ocean,

changing of the tides

refracting the glow
     as if filtered through
          a prism. the watercolors
               have unrolled themselves

higher in the sky,
     and now the lush hues
          are speckled with the dark
               silhouettes of the seabirds

that take refuge here,
     gliding on winds
          carried over the sea
               with the rising sun.

it begins

it begins like this:

an exchanging of glances
blazing wildfire blushing
and rising tidal wave emotions

a hushed conversation
that multiplies, disperses like blackbirds
spattering shared golden-hour sunsets

trading whispery secrets
while fingers intertwine ever so timidly
like slow-creeping flowering vines

the mothwing beating
against your moon-bleached ribcage
echoing against your teeth

stolen starlit kisses
fluttering eyelashes, train-crash shock
and the free-fall love that follows

sunflowers

I crave your warmth
the way sunflowers crave the sun,
ever stretching up to reach
the unreachable.

just as the sunflower grows,
I too reach for your light.

sandcastles

you and I. we
rise with the sun and slip away
to the shore again, let
yesterday's footprints lead us
to the frothy emerald swell
of the first waves to sparkle
with the gilded dawn.
drag the rusty red bucket
up the beach once more
my darling. (do try not to disturb
the gulls). I will scour the sand
for trinkets, driftwood, the lovely
seashells delighting in their varieties
of beige and fawn, coral, amethyst,
blush and rose and cream and ivory.
we built magnificent sandcastles,
you and I. all
grand rising towers and turrets
and moats and drawbridges.
smooth the rough sand into
the same familiar shapes, let
the muscle memory guide us,
fulfill the same promises
as yesterday and the day before
and all the days that linger
in our wake.

YOUR HAND BRUSHES
AGAINST MINE
AND MY HEART SKIPS:

LIKE A STONE ACROSS WATER,
LIKE A NEEDLE ACROSS
A BROKEN RECORD.

stargazing

the freckles brushed across your nose
shatter like stardust, a smattering
of undiscovered constellations.

I think I'll name them all someday.

constellations

invisible lines connect us;
we are a moonlit constellation
and I'm certain
that someone somewhere
charts the movement of our
celestial bodies through a telescope.

pull me into your arms, gravity,
inertia, our twin moons push and pull like the tides.

together,
we will form all the constellations in the galaxy.

dawn

just as I fall, you rise again
with the morning sun that peeks
between the gap-toothed blinds
and washes our cozy bed in light.
with the easiness of routine
you plant a kiss on my forehead
emerging from the nest
of blankets, warmed by new light.
in my uneasy rest, a dreamy mind
wanders to mythology, the stories
of apollo and artemis, the so-called
feminine energy of the cyclical moon.
unlike artemis, I want to inhabit
the same world you do, the one awash
in golden light instead of shadow.
until then, I'm content to share
this moment together at dawn.

I think of you

I think of you / in the depths of a warm conversation / and the shallows of small talk, when / the phone rings / and I neglect to answer (another addition / to the ever-looming pile of voicemails). / I think of you / when I'm waist-deep / floating on the waves, when / the surf greets the sand / and the waves wash over my feet. / I think of you / with the changing of the leaves: I see you / in their golden ambers, dripping sunlight; / in their finest crimsons and ruby reds / that stole your breath / so many autumns ago. / I think of you / as the sun dips behind / the indigo haze of the mountains / and I watch the light fade, slip into / the liminal space between / this dwindling twilight and tomorrow's sleepy dawn. / I think of you / sipping the same mint tea / from the same dainty chipped teacup, / floral-patterned and century-worn, / as you watch the light fade, and we slip / into the liminal space between / the present and the thousand tiny deaths of future.

you kiss me like I'm oxygen
and your lungs are burning for air

grammar lessons

you: an exclamation!
me: a run on sentence of a girl,
a bitten down tongue
unwinding around an ampersand.
us: discovering new syntaxes,
creating something all our own.
this: a language only we understand.

journal entry on some seaside afternoon

how beautiful indeed, this grand, perplexing little thing
we call life.
how astonishing indeed that I can sit here next to you
and feel so complete.
how wonderful indeed to find myself here in this moment
with you.

phases

I tiptoe between
two places
never quite feeling
as though I
belong
(anywhere)
it's just a phase
(or so they whispered)

but I felt more complete than the full moon
as my hand brushed against hers
on that moonlit night;
magic as the moon shadows
creeping over her lips
and burrowing in her dusk-swept eyelashes.

I feel myself wax and wane,
grow full, then become new again.

all they see are phases
of the moon.

in another life

in another life, this is the life we would live:
the two of us in this golden glow,
this warmth beyond all cold.
this is the way we feel in my dreams,
and I imagine maybe in yours too—
the two of us, and no one else,
hidden away between the dunes,
wrapped in our own cocoon
of love, this love, and woven blankets.
I'm constantly battling this feeling.
I want to savor every moment with you,
to take in every second, to memorize
the arrangement of blues and greens
in your eyes, the pattern of your breathing.

no one makes me want to pick up a pen
like you do.

bubblegum

I love the way your name feels on my tongue,
the way it raps its knuckles behind my teeth.
I clench my jaws around the consonants,
push the vowels between my tongue
and the roof of my mouth, letting
delicate words ring against my soft palate.
I chew these words thoughtfully,
try to extract the taste of the syllables,
soft and sweet as bubblegum.
if I could smooth out all the ridges
and keep chewing forever, I would—
until my jaws ache, until my teeth crack—
but I stop short every time to bring my tongue
down from the roof of my mouth,
wrapping my lips around the word *love*.

riptide love

in your eyes,
I catch glimpses of
our endless possibilities
in my hands like fireflies.
in my eyes, your depths rival
that of oceans, that of everything.
getting swept away with the current
is near impossible to avoid. but here I
am, ignoring my better judgment, caught
in this riptide love once again. but I don't mind.

not one bit.

I find myself looking for you
over every horizon

duality

to be with you is to shout
over the crashing waves,
to stare down a monsoon,
to dive headfirst into
a tsunami.

to be with you is to curl
like looping calligraphy,
to slide into a cozy sweater
that already knows the contours
of my body.

it's hard, this thing called love,
but it's always easy loving you.

the color of love

red — your hungry tongue, pressing solace into my skin
orange — your favorite color, sticky sweet on my lips
yellow — our love shines brighter than the midday sun
green — like budding plants, in your arms I sprout anew
blue — the shallow pools of your irises, I dive in again
indigo — the mountains witnessing our sacred moments
violet — flowers you gave me, wilting on the windowsill

between

perhaps somewhere
    between
this horizon and the next, we'll find ourselves
    between
the lolling shimmering waves, or tucked
    between
the melting dunes, slipping silently
    between
the pearly grains of sand,
    between
the cautious sighs of an hourglass.

the dolphins

grey fins cut steel knife-steady against a foaming sea,
rising and falling and all the while, beaming.
I am nearby, suspended in waves and suspense,
bobbing and rolling and all the while, beaming.
the dolphins slip through the waves, ascending
as if star-bound, if only for a moment.
as for me, I am living in slow motion, taking in
the sheer awe of the wildness of the dolphins,
caught in between something like terror and excitement,
wondering how it must feel to be so unmistakably
free.

YOU ARE THE SUN
AND I A LOWLY PLANET

ENDLESSLY REVOLVING
AROUND YOU...

love letters

I keep them in a box
with your CD, you know the one,
the one with all the songs
you wrote for me,
which I, in turn, pretend to like.
this is the sanctuary I keep.
this is the place I guard
the pieces of your heart
that you've gifted to me:
notes passed between classes
(and couriers),
a pen, from a matching set
(you have the other),
a broken locket
(I've been meaning to fix it),
a keychain, two rings,
polaroids, the CD (of course),
and the most precious of all
these treasures: the love letters.
I give you poems in return,
which you, in turn, pretend to like.

something like a miracle

falling in love with you was easy. looking back, I think it was the easiest thing I've ever done. it was all sly smiles across the room, sharing songs, doodles on the back of passed notes. it was little moments of bated breath we shrugged off as meaningless, as if we didn't both hope and wish and pray for what was to come. it was nights spent trying to touch the stars with our toes, pushing each other on swings in a neighborhood park neither of us lived in. it was you writing me songs and me writing you poetry. it was laps and laps on back roads that we thought we could circle forever. it was promises not yet broken and breathless conversations. it was something like a miracle. and oh, how we burned. how brightly we burned.

before the fire consumed us

at some point, we both realized
that to be without each other
was to be without oxygen.

this is how we kept the fire
from going out.

this is how we kept
burning and burning,

licking flames from our fingertips
as if they weren't the very same thing
eating us alive.

after the smoke clears

I want to believe
in our magic.

I want to believe
that somewhere, two people just like us
overcame the obstacles we couldn't
overcome.

I want to believe
that we are not just star-crossed,
but the stars haven't aligned just right
just yet.

I want to believe
in what we had, in what we could have had,
that we can still be something more
than a memory.

I want to believe
we were magic.

I loved you like I love the ocean
which is to say
I understood you were dangerous
and loved you all the more for it

if only

if only
I could devour
your honeycomb words
feel the peach juice
sticky sweet
dribbling down my chin
lick the powdered sugar
from my fingertips

if only
(just once more)
I would go hungry
for a lifetime

poetry in everything

there is poetry in everything: / the way the forks always seem
to need washing before the spoons / the way we pull into
traffic at the last possible second / the way the rain patters on
your roof in its quest to cleanse the earth / the way rainbows
smile across the sky after storms have passed / the way your
favorite home-cooked meal smells after a long day / the way
you always seem to slip unnoticed into my dreams / the way
your scent lingers after you've left / the way your favorite
songs always seem to come on the radio when I'm trying my
best not to think about you / the way all of the poems I write
always end up being about you / you / you.

just as it always promised

i.

the realization that I am no longer in love with you
came slowly, tiptoed along unnoticed before
crashing over me like a tidal wave,
swallowing me up in the rising seawater.
it was a feeling that preferred to go unnoticed,
much like the unassuming gentle waves
that precede a tsunami.

ii.

as wonderful as the high tide was,
we shouldn't have ignored its threats
to swell and overtake us,
to carry us out to sea,
to swallow us whole.

it crept up on us,
just as it always promised.

changing of the tides

emma conlon

low tide

the same stale air

you tell me my heart has gotten too big again
so you cut it out of my ribs, place it gingerly

on the coffee table. what a heavy, ugly thing
it is, and yet it still beats, convulsing

like a wounded animal between the pages of
the perpetually open coffee table book

you've been "meaning to read" for 2 years.
and then: the familiar swish of a switch

blade slicing open the same stale air.
you take my heart in your hands,

all wild and swollen and hissing, whittle
it down to something more palatable, something

you wouldn't mind displaying next to
the perpetually open coffee table book

you've been "meaning to read" for 2 years.
your practiced hands slice away at the writhing

monstrosity until it is something slight
and unrecognizable, no less offensive

than a hangnail. meanwhile, you're wondering
how the damned thing got to be so big

in the first place. meanwhile, I'm wondering
how many pieces of me you can take

before I am no longer myself.

never mind

I love you
we exhaled to the universe
over and over again
until the day came
that you said
I don't love you anymore

I guess what you meant to say was
never mind

and so it goes

and so
the record stops turning
you lift the needle
I put the album on the shelf

and so
the latch resets
you close the door
I lock it behind you

WHEN YOU LEFT
YOU TOOK A PART OF ME
WITH YOU

THERE IS A HOLE IN MY CHEST
AS BIG AS AN OCEAN

and nothing can fix it but you

anchor

you were supposed to hold me steady against the waves.
you were supposed to ground me in this turbulence.
you were supposed to be my anchor.
(you promised. you *promised*.)
so I *suppose*
I'm wondering
when it was
you decided
to drown me
instead.

you gave me artificial flowers

there was something about us
that was artificial—
diet cola, chemically synthesized,
something a bit too good to be true,
a zero calorie sweetener.

the first glance, the first taste: sweet.
but you left, left me alone with the sour
aftertaste, aspartame,
saccharin, sucralose,
little paper packets
of pink or blue or yellow
you shuffled between your fingers
like playing cards.

there's nothing you can do to nurture artificial love.
at least artificial flowers never wilt.

nothing lasts

i.

our love was sweet,
soft,
like the ice cream
we ate together
on summer afternoons,

one hand on the cone,
the other reaching,
always reaching for you.

ii.

I could never hold you
in my hands for long
before you melted away,
leaving me
with a broken heart,
sticky hands,
and melted ice cream.

do you remember

do you remember the night we held the stars?
how odd it was indeed
to have galaxies within our reach
solar systems balanced on our fingertips

I can still feel your light
the warmth of your skin against mine
even as I grow colder
with each passing day

just like the stars
you had me in your grasp
(though I could never seem
to get a hold of you)

just like the stars
we burned ever so bright
(though in time you tried
to extinguish my flame)

just like the stars
we were destined to die.

I can't listen to the same songs anymore

to listen to them is to think of you,
to teleport back to moments
that have since slipped through our fingers.

the moment we unlaced
our fingers from each other's grasp
was the moment we let the love
fall through the cracks.

WHAT WE CALLED
"LOVE"
WOULD BE BETTER NAMED
"OBSESSION"

wash you out of my hair

the smell of you
has been tangled up in my hair for weeks
your touch
still lingers on my skin
no matter how many times I
shampoo
and rinse
and repeat
I still can't seem to cleanse myself of you

your phantom fingers still run through my hair
(shampoo and rinse and repeat)
I still feel the warmth your lips left on my cheek
(shampoo and rinse and repeat)
I swear I hear you whispering my name in the dark
(shampoo and rinse and repeat
shampoo and rinse and repeat
shampoo and rinse and repeat...)

perforated edges

I can't help but be wary
of the perforated edges
that lay between us.
we may still be attached,
but it feels far too easy
for you to rip me out,
toss me aside,
rewrite our story.

even the shoreline changes

on the nights that sleep eludes me
or plays me cool and coy as a cat,
the winds in my mind fill my sails
and send me across the sea to you.

it's nights like these when stillness
shakes my bones that I wonder how
you convinced me our love was forever—
nothing is.

even the shoreline changes
with the exhalation of passing waves.
even the stars that guide us
collapse to dust before we see their light.
even the suredness of land
is a steady illusion, millenia-drifting.

time is a tricky mistress, and fate
cannot be caught between your palms.

even the shoreline shifts
in time.

the dark / the light

maybe it wasn't your love that I craved
so desperately in our final days together.
perhaps I had grown so accustomed to the dark
that the light was an even greater betrayal.

I may have lit the match
but it was you who burned us down

five days

there's only five more days to go / and I'm telling myself that
I can do this / I'm telling myself we can make it through this /
but you're making it hard / you're making it impossible /
you're making it insufferable / and I'm suffocating trying to
breathe / this stagnant air / because neither of us / will open
the windows out of spite / so we both sit across the table /
stealing ragged breaths / averting our eyes / scratching our
dinner plates with our forks / because it's the easiest way to
break the silence / we're wilting in the silence / we're
wondering how it got like this / we're mumbling meaningless
words / in languages neither of us speak / because there is an
ocean between us / and we are terrified to say anything wrong
/ lest it open up and swallow us whole / we're standing on
opposite shores / hoping our smoke signals will curl / over the
curve of the horizon / because we don't have ships / and we
don't want to swim / and / and / and / we both think it's the
other's responsibility / to reach the other side / so now / the
only thing we ever do together / is watch the clock run out.

chess

it was always a game to you
wasn't it?
and sometimes, something nobler still:
you, the mighty intellect,
me, the less-than-worthy challenger,
reduced to an obstacle
reflected in your pride-glazed eyes.

we waltzed again,
all swinging feet and jabbing elbows
and crashing plates and screeching tires
and bleeding feet and burning rubber.
(and even then)
time after time I sacrificed my queen
for a king who could not shed a tear for her.

how odd indeed to hold a wooden game piece
and see instead a piece of myself, saltwater-warped,
never again fitting quite the same way it did before.

in any case, I broke the chess board in half
like you did me. see, I have learned something
in spite of you.

your move.

NOTHING IS FAIR
WHEN LOVE BECOMES WAR

holy ground

how dare you desecrate
the temple I welcomed you into
with open arms

didn't you know you were on holy ground?

circle the drain

I take comfort in knowing this skin
has never been touched by him, that the cells
his fingers grazed have since been shed
just as I have shed him, like an old winter coat
or an exoskeleton. it must go for me to grow.
I have scrubbed the memory of him
from between my fingernails until they bled.
I have sat in the boiling shower and scrubbed
myself raw, watching any trace of me
that he may recognize
circle the drain.

MAYBE ANYTHING
LOOKS LIKE LOVE
IF YOU'RE LONELY
ENOUGH

floating

I'm floating
without a life jacket
in the middle of the ocean,
wondering when I'll give in again
to the sinking.
there is no land in sight,
but I can see the clouds shift
as the world keeps turning without me.
I can sense the sharks that swim beneath me,
but I know they won't bother me—
not yet. not now.

every so often, I see boats in the distance,
but I don't bother flagging them down.
not anymore.
besides,
my arms are tired
of treading water,
my lungs exhausted
from screaming for help
to people who can't hear me.

it's not that I want to drown,
I just accept it as a possibility.
and sure,
I've tied anchors to my swollen feet
and plunged head first before,

but invisible hands inevitably
hoist me from the depths.
besides,

I wouldn't call it drowning,
not anymore.
but treading water is leaching
the life out of me, osmosing
out to the salt water I call home.
so now
I'm floating
without a life jacket
in the middle of the ocean,
wondering if I'll ever find
the strength to swim to shore.

monster

I'm sorry
I know the right words escape you
and frankly
I myself don't even know
what's left to say

I've stripped this universe down
torn galaxies to pieces
with my shaking hands
but I don't feel strong
I feel ashamed

(here lies a girl:
destroyer of worlds,
destroyer of herself,
harbinger of her own demise,
etc., etc....)

I've felt every knife-twist word
in my skin
and kept twisting
anyway

anxiety

I know you.
I know you all too well.

I know the way
you scratch and claw your way
to the forefront of an uneasy mind,
lacing your icy fingers through
the webs of veins and arteries.

I know the way
you stalk me like a shadow
or a vicious predator closing in on its prey,
the serpentine constriction winding
around my collapsing ribs.

I know the way
you force my lungs to contract
and tighten, my heart to drop to my feet.
the way the blood boils hot
then slows, molasses-thick.

I know you.
I know you all too well.

you are not some unrecognizable beast,
but rather, an old acquaintance
who comes knocking at inconvenient hours,
flashing your sharp-toothed grin
and slipping in when I crack open the door
to see who's there. you're no stranger,
but you are not the friend
that you pretend to be.

sunken

some days, I scream with all
the might I can muster

from where I sit at the bottom
of this dark and unforgiving sea,

among the ghostly graveyards
of ships and sharks and sunken treasures.

the bubbles escaping my lungs break
to a tranquil surface, where you sail

blissfully above the waves.
maybe it is better to settle

into the sand, into the comfort
of the eerie silence.

"okay"

my roommate asks me
"are you okay?"
and I do not know how to answer.

I want to ask her what she means
by "okay", what boxes I need to check,
what requirements I need to fulfill,
what standards I need to meet.

I want to ask her, *can I still be okay*
if every breath is a struggle against
the sorrow that sits atop my chest?
can I still be okay if I feel like I'm
slipping underneath a dark rolling sea
that seems too cold and vast to comprehend?
can I still be okay if my depression
has coiled around me like some unrelenting
serpent keen on tightening until I break?

her worry casts long shadows
over the door frame. I tell her,
"I'm feeling introspective",
which is not untrue.
I am deep in thought, buried away
in some unknown cave, unheard, unseen.
what I do not tell her
remains unsaid.

REPENTANCE

(OR, THE LIES I HAVE TOLD)

1. I'M FINE,
2. I PROMISE.
3. DON'T WORRY ABOUT ME,
4. I'LL BE OKAY.
5. I'M GREAT,
6. THANKS FOR ASKING!
7. I'M DOING WELL.
8. I'M FEELING BETTER.
9. I'M NOT UPSET.
10. I DON'T MIND EITHER WAY.
11. I LOVE YOU.
12. I LOVE YOU TOO.
13. I'M OK.
14. I'M OK.
15. I'M OK.

tea (for two)

I suppose that's all this is
isn't it?
an exchanging of niceties
and playing pretend
and screaming in mirrors
belong
belong
belong
(but only when you think no one is looking)

so
we swallow half-truths like teacakes
and sip daintily
as if it doesn't burn our tongues

a stagnant budding

i.

sometimes,
authenticity alarms me.
I don't know why I suppress it,
as desperate to fade into the background
as I am to shine.

ii.

it's funny—at least, I think it's funny—
we never think we've fully blossomed
at any point but the present,
and sometimes, not even then.
we look to the past and say, *aha!*
you were mistaken! but I don't feel
I've blossomed. I can't be sure I will.
like a blooming, paused.
like a stagnant budding.

emma conlon

ocean-bound

I think I've sprung a leak—
the floodgates aren't quite closing.
(god forbid they ever open all the way,
at least not forever—
because sometimes they do. they do.)

this is a slow trickle, the kind
that collects on a mountaintop
and stumbles into streams, collecting
into the rivers that rush ocean-bound.

I am terrified to be ocean-bound.

I am terrified to lose this slippery grip
of control when everything else
glides in unpredictable patterns
past the corners of my vision.

I am terrified of being swept away
with the currents.

I am terrified to be ocean-bound.

requiem

the first time that I thought you had died,
the night had come black velvet heavy
in the absence of the moon. even
the stars struggled to sustain their light.

it was late autumn. the air was cold
in a thick sort of way that seemed to
permeate the skin and settle in
to bone. seeping dread began to gnaw

the lining of my stomach. somehow,
I sensed disruption. the call confirmed
this; the story spun dizzily forward.
the fog on my window was the only sign

I was still breathing. I looked to the stars
for a sign. they held their breath with me.

lessons in being lonely

spend all your time in books / jot down little notes in the margins / daydream / (often) / find comfort in your solitude / (whatever form that takes) / take long showers / unless you're sad / or, conversely, especially if you're sad / try not to overthink / specifically during the aforementioned showers / unless you're sad / or, conversely, especially if you're sad / avoid the urge to descend into the social media abyss / (descend anyway) / call an old friend / hang up before they can answer / peruse used book store aisles / be ready to fake a smile / and force conversation / with the employee who always asks / "can I help you with anything?" / because there is so much you need help with / and so little anyone can actually help you with

a haunting

i.

in a dream, I'm chained to an anchor,
trapped on the ocean floor, trapped
in miles and miles of darkness.
you are the light shining from the surface.

ii.

in a dream, the saltwater never
stings my eyes. deep down I know
this ocean is my own creation,
a sea of lonesome saltwater tears.

iii.

in a dream, I saw you as a ghost
of the person you once were.
I think I should call this an omen.
instead, I call it a haunting.

jellyfish

I wanted to be like you,

you know?
I envied the way you floated
aimlessly through it all,
the way you let the currents
carry you wherever they went,
wherever they saw fit.

you know,
I envied your indifference
as I waged wars with waves,
envied your driftwood ease
as I struggled against the tides,
struggled to stay afloat.

you said
I could be like you, if only I would let you in.
still, you stung me every time I tried to hold you.

nocturne

a plane flies overhead at 2 am
and I am struck suddenly by
the unexpected disruption, the way it
shattered the silence that had settled
on my skin in tepid layers.
I realize that perhaps the silence
was nothing more than an illusion
as I'm briskly reacquainted
with the ambient soundscape:
the humming of the fan motor,
the whirring of its blades,
the inexplicable creaking of the house
as ghosts pass through the walls
(or maybe something more mundane,
perhaps the restless shifting of old pipes),
the near incessant chirping
of crickets outside my window,
and now the sliding of my hand
across paper, recording this composition,
this nighttime symphony
I had never seemed to notice—
just as I hadn't noticed
the gentle sound of your breathing
until it was no longer there.

da capo al fine

in some ways,
you always feel the same.

your eyes are still the same
wandering cloud pale blue,
the constellations of freckles
shatter like stardust in the same
familiar patterns they always have.

still,
you've changed.

"you've changed."
you set these words down politely
over the rim of your coffee cup,
nestled between a sigh and a sip
of what I assume is your fourth cup today.
you used to have your fourth cup
around this time of day, when the sun
peeked through the curtains at just
the right angle to set your room aglow.
"I'm not saying that's a bad thing…"
your hair is darker than I remember.

changing of the tides

in some ways,
we feel like strangers.

your eyes are still the same
wandering cloud pale blue,
but the light within has faded.
I think I may have trapped you
in the amber haze of a memory.

still,
you've changed.

I'm still writing you letters all these years later
I guess part of me still misses you
in spite of everything

the words I gave to you

you are the sun
and I a lowly planet

how foolish I was
to reduce myself
to a life of revolving around you
when I have breathed life
where you have burned

even if I am a planet
you are not the only star
in all the cosmos

precognition

the news that you are engaged
does not upset me as much
as I think it should. truthfully,
it does not upset me at all.

I could write a thousand poems
about what this means.

instead, I think about the
not-so-distant past, the one in which
you described visions in which we met
at the end of a wedding aisle.

I could write a thousand more poems
about what this means.

in spite of everything, I'm glad
your plan is working out for you.
I had always suspected your visions
had little to do with me anyway.

the only thing I'm sorry for
is pretending to see that future too.

brick by brick

you built me up
brick by brick
and I was so grateful
I turned a blind eye
when you instead began
building walls around me.

by the time I realized
you were sealing me inside,
it was too late;
the final brick was laid.

when I found the strength
to break through your walls,
you didn't hesitate
to tear me down
brick by brick.

that's ok—I have good foundations.
I'll rebuild myself in my own image

brick
by
brick.

mosaic

I may be broken
shattered
damaged
cracked
and bruised
but even broken pieces
can be rearranged into
something new
something beautiful

changing of the tides

emma conlon

changing
tides

how I will survive

I will collect beautiful things
from the spaces between tragedies

I will fill the cracks
on my porcelain heart with gold

I will write these words
even when I don't feel brave

this is how I will survive

this too was a miracle

falling in love with you was easy.
falling out of love was harder, but
this too was a miracle.

your lips have never known

I'm teaching myself
to keep *I'm sorry* in my chest
instead of letting it spill
and fill the space like *um* and *uh*.

I'm teaching myself
that my existence isn't a sin,
that my every inhalation doesn't
mandate an exhaled atonement.

this isn't something
I expect you to understand.
your lips have never known
the taste of apology.

MIRROR, MIRROR...

I pray one day
I will greet this body as a home
instead of a prison

enough

I'm tired of never feeling
enough
not smart enough
not pretty enough
not thin enough
not strong enough
not good enough

these hands
can move mountains
these legs
can make the longest journey
these lips
can breathe life anew

who are you to tell me what I'm worth?

with these hands
I will move mountains
with these legs
I will make the longest journey
with these lips
I will breathe life anew

I am enough.
I am enough.
I am enough.

HEALING IS A JOURNEY

I am not there yet,
but god, I want to get there.
I have to get there.

HEALING IS A JOURNEY II

admittedly, this
journey is longer than I
anticipated.

author's note

I write as a way of healing,
a way of taking the sorrows rising in these bones
and spinning them into something like gold,
a way of stitching together wounds
with my own two broken hands,
a way of tracing along my spiderweb scars
and finding something magic in myself.

I am learning to be a poet

by:

introducing myself to ghosts / listening to what they have to say / searching for beauty in the mundane / throwing caution to the wind, and then / shutting the windows, and then / opening them back up anyway / trying my best to know myself / trying harder to know others / writing love letters / burning love letters / wondering if burning love letters is bad for the environment / googling "is burning paper bad for the environment?" / asking questions / asking the questions I want answered / writing until my hands shake / steadying said hands, writing more / and more / and more / letting my heart ache / even when it is inconvenient / especially when it is inconvenient

MY ENGLISH TEACHERS
ALWAYS TOLD ME THERE WAS
A DIFFERENCE BETWEEN
THE SPEAKER AND THE POET
BUT I SWEAR SOMETIMES
WE ARE ONE AND THE SAME!

wildflowers

I will let myself grow
        and grow
                and grow
even in the places—
especially in the places—
I am learning to love.

I will plant the seeds of self-love
in the garden of my aching soul
until my heart overflows
with wildflowers.

freckles

growing up, I never liked
my freckles. imperfect, accidental,
as if some unknowable being spilled
cinnamon sugar across my face.
but the universe took care
with every thoughtful brushstroke—
each freckle dusting the bridge
of my nose and dispersing along
my cheekbones is
purposeful. intentional.
in my reflection I see
constellations, combusting nebulae
that traveled lightyears to teach me
there is beauty in the imperfections.

I am

I am an unlit match:
something dangerous in the wrong hands—
proceed with caution, danger ahead!
a titaness who freed herself
you fear, revere, suppress, conceal,
scorched earth and burning embers.

I am a butterfly wing:
something to be handled with care—
fragile stickers, postage stamps,
an unraveling sweater
you can't seem to help but pick at,
threads whisked away by the wind.

ode to my stretch marks

your lightning bolt ferocity cracks across my skin,
sending shockwaves through me as I inspect you.
my fingers travel over the pink-scarred topography:
mountain ranges, rivers winding through canyons,
brooks and streams and creeks of a watershed map.

like the rings that circle through tree trunks,
you too remind me that I am still growing.

bow and arrow

if I am to be anything, let me be an arrow
so that every time anyone dares pull me back
I propel forward in search of better things

sidewalk gardens

look for love in the most unlikely places.
you'll be surprised at what you'll find.

much like the flowers that grow
in the cracks in the sidewalk,
beauty can be found in unexpected places
if you're only willing to look.

black coffee

every person I have ever loved drank black coffee
every morning, locked-in like clockwork,
sometimes more:
two, three, four times each day.

the first two left me
with the bitter taste
lingering on my lips,
endlessly scrubbing coffee grounds
from beneath my fingernails.

the third taught me
to love the taste of black coffee
for all its bitterness, for all
its richness. to love the strength
of coffee, of love's unwithering embrace.

there is a lesson to be learned
here, as in most things.

you will learn to love again.

reminder

you are a work in progress.
you will not be rushed.
give yourself the time you need
to grow.

after all,
even the humble caterpillar takes her time
before she emerges a butterfly.

reminder ii

and dearest, don't forget
to tuck the wondrous things
safely away, to treasure each
small gift from the universe.
press the flowers blooming in your soul
between the pages of old books.
fold up the lovely moments
and stick them in your pocket
so that maybe wandering fingers
will unearth that precious magic
when you need it most.

I'll be your mirror

I've poured myself into broken bottles,
into empty things with holes in the bottoms,
watched pieces of myself slip through oil-slick fingers
and wash down storm drains.

I've pieced together shattered glass fragments
with scotch tape and crossed fingers, never mind
the times I cut myself on sharp edges
and sharper tongues.

I've given away pieces of myself to fill up others,
to make the broken whole again, to mend
the things that can't be mended, to patch
the things that won't be patched.

wounds will not be willed into healing.
this I know. still, I've never minded being a mirror.

you are so much more than what they think
you are so much more than you know

you are all the stars in the cosmos
you are a bright and beautiful thing

kindness

when I was young, my mother held me in her lap and told me to always be kind. and I've tried, as best as I was able. I absorbed these hallowed words, handled them with care, tucked them away somewhere safe, etched them in stone over and over again like a commandment. when my heart beat sorrow and my blood was thick with anger, I wasn't always kind. I fell prey to the hurting, tried to make you hurt the way you hurt me. regret weighs heavy, but neither of us can take away the things we said in anger, in pain. I can still feel the scars that those sharp words left on my tongue. they'll always linger—the mind heals, but it never forgets. I've shed a tear for every unkind word I've spoken; each malice-laden syllable that has burst forth like fire from my cracked and bleeding lips weighs heavy against the feather of truth. maybe I will always feel monstrous regret pushing down on my chest, staring deep into my weary eyes as if to say *look what you've become.* sometimes it's so heavy that every breath is an absurd labor: I am sisyphus pushing my rock to the peak of the mountain only to watch it roll back down, a cruel erasure of my strife. yet just last week you looked at me with that honey-drenched smile and told me you loved me because I was so *kind.* those simple words washed over me like a warm tide on the shore. such is the power of kindness. I drank sweet nectar from the flowers that bloomed in my soul, feasted on your ambrosia words. and I sang. I sang. *I sang.* because kindness is all I want to put out into the universe. it is all that I aspire to be. I know there is not a return policy for cruelty.

I know scars may fade, but they can never be erased. the wounds remain. I know that there is finality in even the most trivial of words. these are the lessons we all learn. nothing can reverse the pain we've caused, but god, I hope you were right.

there is nothing I want more than to be kind.

emma conlon

places I've searched for myself

tea leaves / tarot cards / open windows / closed doors / my
father's face / my mother's laughter / my nana's garden / the
woods beyond / museum gift shops / thrift shop aisles / used
book stores / library shelves / spoken word / words unspoken /
newspaper headlines / love letters / mix tapes / songs on the
radio / unsung melodies / mirrors / the backs of spoons / storm
clouds / the rainbows that follow / rooftops / cigarette smoke /
around corners / behind microphones / in spotlights / under
moonlight / under covers / (under cover) / dusty attics / photo
albums / through car windows / the backs of taxis / between
exhales / between moments / in your arms / in your eyes / you.

november 24th, 2019

I remember the waves the most, the way they rose turquoise and vicious in the salted wind and crashed with foamy ivory ease as we sat there on the shore, alone, together, and very much in love. I remember the waves, and how strangely cold the sand was even as it smolder-glowed warm and golden in the expiring sunshine. maybe more than the waves, I remember the laughter, and I remember how it warmed us on that chilly november seaside afternoon.

YOURS ARE NOT
THE ONLY HANDS
THAT HAVE TRIED
TO HOLD ME,
BUT YOURS FEEL
THE MOST LIKE HOME.

home

I always thought that home
was somewhere I could point to on a map,
a place with a street number,
an address, a mailbox,
a house with brick walls and bay windows
pouring sunshine like lemon cream
through lace heirloom curtains,
speckling the cherrywood floors of a cozy kitchen,
warm and cinnamon-sugar sweet,
filled with framed photos of dimpled children,
a curated collection of memories
lining honeysuckle walls like the crooked teeth
of a familiar loving smile.

but no house will ever feel as much like home
as you do
because home is not a place,
but a feeling,
a comfort.
and even without a deadbolt to secure,
a latch to pull, a lock and key,
your arms are still my safest place.
I'll always be able to find my way home
to you.

small things

love, sometimes it's the small things.
this isn't all grand gestures
and rose petals and kissing in the rain.
this isn't all waxing and waxing poetic,
romantic monologues and declarations
of a love unwithering, a love eternal.
it's the warmth of your skin against mine
and the gentle way you wipe away my tears.
it isn't just the hallmark card words, it's
the words we barely choke out in the thick
of full-bellied laughter, the words
we whisper in the quiet of the night.
it's my face in your hands. the little texts
letting me know you're thinking of me.
the "just because" flowers. the sheer
wonderment of rising with the sun
and rediscovering the indescribable joy
of waking next to the person you love.

ocean-heart

I've tried to tame
this wild ocean-heart of mine
well before I tried to pour it
into your outstretched hands.

I know I'm a lot to handle.
this wild ocean-heart of mine
isn't always calm; it has its storms.
everything passes in time.

the waves have their ways.
this wild ocean-heart of mine
can swallow ships whole
and rock sailors gently to sleep.

the tides may rise and fall in
this wild ocean-heart of mine,
but through it all, I know
they will change again.

and yet, here you stand.
despite the waves.
despite the storms.
despite the tides.

changing of the tides

i. by sun

I follow your footsteps down to the shore,
your golden hair waving in the sea breeze.
you sway with the crashing waves
and smile, dimpling those sandy freckles
that speckle your face, a constellation
softened by time—
sand trickling through an hourglass.
these precious hours we spend
unearthing poseidon's hidden treasures:
flotsam, jetsam,
seaglass and shark teeth,
pretty bits of twine
twirling through pink seashell fingertips,
tangible, intangible bonds,
sailing knots that tie us together,
like this, you say—just so.
you draw me in with those tide pool eyes
and I test the waters, dip a toe in
hoping to steal a glimpse
of starfish, sea snails,
fish flickering in those shallow depths.
but again I lean in too close,
the ripples giving way to frenzied splash
as we fall into each other once more,
sending sculpins scuttling for cover.

changing of the tides

i. by moon

dreams float, soft as seafoam,
gulls on the wind.
your breath is steady as the tide.
crests and troughs, you rise and fall
with the waves beyond the milky white
salt-battered windows.
in sleep, your stormy seas are calm,
illuminated by moonbeams
stealing through the gauzy curtains.
I paint this scene in my mind in
swirling watercolor blues and greens.
you stir, and bring me close to you—
I am complete again.
as eyelids grow heavy with sand,
I reflect on those stolen nights
we spent together in the dunes,
soft sand still warm between our toes
as you guided me through rippling grass,
moonlight reflected on the dark water
of your eyes, gentle as the midnight tide.
you dried my ocean-water tears
with every moonlit smile;
sail away, sail away sailor—
I still think of you every time
I shake the sand from my shoes.

love in the end of times

march 23rd, 2020

like most people, I find myself taking stock
of the things that are truly important
in these so-called end of times.
like most people, I'm finding this exercise
to be exhausting. they say reward will come
in time, but then again, they also say
we're running out of it.
I'm trying to be forgiving of myself, especially
in these so-called end of times.
I'm trying to be more forgiving of you too.

and here you are: the solitary life preserver
in the sea of things-that-want-to-kill-me,
offering your safe harbor—whatever that means
in these so-called end of times.
I'm inclined to take the bait, to wait it out
underneath your sea of warm blankets,
to carve out a space for myself within your chest,
to wait for this storm to pass,
to wait for the light to come.

warrior

when I was a shipwreck of a girl, I caught
a glimpse of my reflection in the rolling water.
somewhere behind my splintered eyes
I found the strength to rise from the wreckage.

through the murkiness of stormy seas,
swirling in my depths there is a warrior;
strong enough to fight my own demons,
brave enough to win my own battles.

I spent so long waiting for someone to save me
I forgot I was capable of saving myself.

bad poetry

when they ask, I say
"I write bad poetry",
which is a joke. but mostly, it isn't.
which is to say I know I can't expect
anyone to believe in me
when I don't believe in myself.
which is to say I'm learning.
I'm learning.
slow-burn-whiskey-learning.
newborn-fawn-wobble-learning.
so call it what you will.
I'll call it growth.
I'll call it healing.
I'll call it love.

I'M LEARNING:

1. To love myself
2. To forgive you
3. I will always,
    always be learning.

perennials

flowers always seem to know
when it's their time to die
and make room for their children.
the wilt and rot will nourish
the seeds that grow from its grave.

just as the moon expands
so she can wither away again,

just as the tides creep up
and down the shores eternally,

just as new love rises like a
phoenix from the ashes of that

which came before. not an end,
but perennial beginnings.

calliope taps me on the shoulder

a poem has been rattling around my head for weeks.

it knocks over plates and rummages through silverware.
it sifts through my notebooks and sighs into the curtains.
it echoes in the pipes and tiptoes over creaking floorboards.
it raps on my windows at night, then morphs into branches.
it weaves trails of clues to let me know it has arrived,
then hides in a cupboard and bids me to seek it.

today, you asked me a question and the poem answered.

in this way, the poem is an intruder, a mischievous
neighbor who calls the open window an invitation.
the poem invites itself to stay despite my protestations
that it is too early, too late, that it must come again later,
and yet, when I ask the poem to lunch, or to have tea,
the poem is gone, and leaves no forwarding address.

sometimes it welcomes me, sometimes it shakes a fist at me.

it greets me at the door, winding around my legs like a cat,
or else it shatters the mirrors, rips the paintings from the wall.
it leaves me love letters and scrawls angry notes on napkins,
whispers in my ear as I sleep and wakes me in the morning.
much like the tides, the poem and I have our ebbs, our flows.
still, I hope the poem will one day make a home out of me.

conversations with the girl in the mirror

she points at the blooming violet crescents
underneath my eyes, pinches my stomach
between her fingers, tugs at my skin
as if to excavate something new beneath.
she tries to mold flesh into strange new shapes.
she picks and prods at the things she calls
imperfections, traces stretch marks, runs
smooth fingertips over stubborn scars.
she says, _how will I learn?_
I say, _we will learn together._

changing of the tides

emma conlon

acknowledgements

Thank you to every English teacher I have ever had for helping to shape me into the person I am today. Thank you especially to Ms. Pace and Ms. Edelman; your classrooms were a safe haven in an extremely difficult time in my life, and for that I am forever grateful.

Thank you to Professor Laurie Kutchins for reigniting my love for writing, and to all of my classmates and workshop partners who read many of these poems in their youngest and messiest forms. Without your insights, these poems would not be what they are today.

Thank you to my friends and family who supported me through this process and encouraged me to actually sit down and publish this collection: my parents; my sisters, Michaela and Claire; my friends and earliest readers, Sarah, Angeline, Mak, and Lauren; and my wonderful partner Reid. I could not (and likely would not) have done it without you.

Lastly, thank you for reading. I'm honored every time someone has any interest in reading something that I wrote. It truly means the world to me.

notes and credits

"coronation" was written for a poetry class in which I was tasked with "apprenticing" and emulating a master poet; I chose Mary Oliver. The structure of the poem is inspired by the structure she uses in her poems "The Hermit Crab" and "White-Eyes", among others.

The first two lines of "the words I gave to you" were taken from a poem I wrote a long time ago for someone I once loved. I have since repurposed them.

"grammar lessons" was inspired by "mistaken" by Alison Malee.

"I am learning to be a poet" was inspired by "how to be a poet" by Chelsea Diane.

The title of the poem on page 43 refers to the song "And So It Goes" by Billy Joel.

The title and final line of the poem on page 108 refers to the song "I'll Be Your Mirror" by The Velvet Underground.

changing of the tides

A few of the poems included in this book were originally written or revised from earlier drafts in response to prompts provided by poets I respect and admire: Savannah Brown ("dawn", "perennials"), Emma Grace Lukens ("mosaic", "the color of love", "home", "nothing lasts", "you gave me artificial flowers", "kindness", "enough", "freckles", "phases", "if only", "author's note", "duality", "the dark / the light", "I can't listen to the same songs anymore"), L.T. Pelle ("after the smoke clears"), and Courtney Phillips ("wash you out of my hair"). These poems have come a long way since I first scribbled them down in a notebook (and some are unrecognizable from their initial incarnations), but many of these poems may never have existed at all if not for these wonderful poets. Thank you for your prompts, and thank you for your art.

"changing of the tides" was the first poem I wrote after years of taking a break from writing poetry. It is also the first poem I ever felt truly proud of, and it inspired me to start sharing my poetry with the world.

emma conlon

about the author

Emma Conlon is a writer and poet currently based in Charlottesville, Virginia. *Changing of the Tides* is her first published poetry collection. She completed her B.A. in English with minors in Creative Writing and Music at James Madison University in 2020, and she is currently pursuing a master's degree at the University of Virginia. When she isn't writing, Emma enjoys traveling, making music, meeting dogs, reading anything she can get her hands on, filling notebooks with doodles, and dreaming up plans that may or may not ever come to fruition.

http://byemmaconlon.wordpress.com

instagram: @byemmaconlon
facebook: @byemmaconlon
tumblr: @emmaconlon

emma conlon

<u>index</u>

changing of the tides

changing of the tides

emma conlon

Made in the USA
Monee, IL
02 April 2022

93967883R20085